The String Theory
Beginning With Me

Story and Illustrations By
Tonia Colleen Martin

Graphic Design By
Jennifer Rose Triebwasser

In the beginning I was chaos.
The light in me mingled with the dark.
I feared what I did not know.
Things seen cannot be unseen.
Things heard cannot be silenced.
Scars cannot migrate to new skin.

And though I walked in circles, curiosity
plagued me. Who is my Maker? I asked.

When it came to animals, I wanted distance.
I feared them. They abounded.

The serpent questioned and threatened.
The majestic lion crept along roaring.

Charismatic birds sang and boasted.
Tiny creatures annoyed and bit.
These all, in their entirety, were at once,
beneath me, incessantly hovering and watching from the sidelines.

A woman sought to comfort me.
But what could she do?
She, herself was afraid –
Even the animal's names frightened her.

And yes, there was a man, but he had secrets as large as her fears.

Together
they
gave
me
an
ancient
key.

He said, "Its door is too tiny for more than one."

The woman agreed. "Doors are shape- shifters," she added.

"Do not trust those with wide and high arches."

Trust the drum in your chest, he said

The man continued. "This key is a magnet, as well as a scribe.
Carry it with an open heart."

Then a gentle canary whispered in my ear, "Trust the drum in your chest."

I protested. "I am a tender ear. I am tiny hands, scraped elbows, bruised knees. My eyes are weak."

But no one remained to hear me.

The key was a heavy treasure.
It sought its home.
It would not relent.
It drew me to the water.
The waves echoed the drum in my chest.
The wind said, "Oh how hard you try."
It drew me to the land. "Your maker is my Maker," it said.
The flowers said, "The one who made us is the one who made you."
The birds said, "Stop worrying."
The sun said, "Pay attention, there is wisdom in that key."
The shade befriended me. "Sit and rest," it said.

I did not trust my eyes.
I did not trust my skittish heart.
I did not trust the world beyond my circles.

Had the shape of the key not imaged my bones I would have traded it for wine.
I would have forged it into wings.
I would have let the jungle chew it to dust.

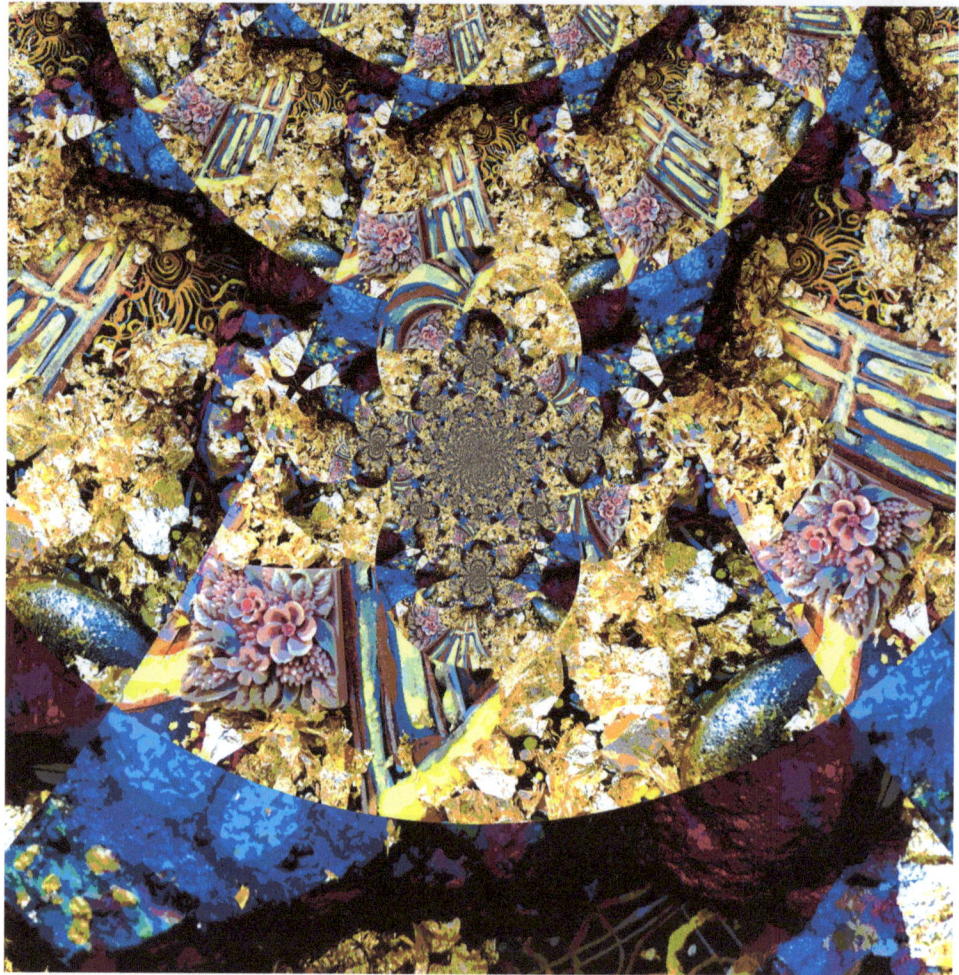

The key increased in weight until the drum in my chest burst.
When the dust cleared,
I saw a arch furrowed by time and etched with promise.
I saw a smoldering threshold.
I saw light layered upon dark.
I saw blood in the mix but it wasn't mine.

I cowered and closed my eyes and when I opened them,
I saw my Maker.

Yahweh stood in the threshold.
Yahweh stood beyond the threshold.
Yahweh stood before the threshold.
There were three of Him and nothing could contain them.

Shouldered by Yahweh's compassion,
I saw myself as a woman of ravines and gullies.
A woman of vistas incomprehensible.
I saw the beauty of my scars.
I heard the message of hope.
I experienced love bigger than my fears.

And Yahweh said, "I'm the drum in your heart."

Tonia Colleen Martin

The String Theory Beginning With Me, an illustrated prose poem, traces the journey to freedom from an internal landscape of chaos and fear. Using specific images from the natural world, this story condenses and simplifies a very slow, methodical transformation indicative of those who consistently seek the larger experience of living both in and beyond the here and now. Because of its metaphorical language and its delicate presentation, *The String Theory Beginning with Me,* has a universal appeal and is an ideal gift for both contemplatives and the spirited.

Other Books in My Collection:

 Having Tried Everything

 About Face

 Rest: A Call To Freedom

 Intents & Purposes

More information about my stories and art can be found at:
www.toniacolleenmartin.com

www.ingramcontent.com/pod-product-compliance
Lightning Source LLC
Chambersburg PA
CBHW042010090426
42811CB00015B/1601